BUSINESS IN THE GILDED AGE

BUSINESS

in

THE GILDED AGE

The Conservatives'
Balance Sheet

———

Edward C. Kirkland

UNIVERSITY OF WISCONSIN PRESS

MADISON – 1952

THE KNAPP LECTURES

IT WAS the express desire of the late Kemper K. Knapp that a part of the income from his bequest to the University of Wisconsin "be used to cultivate in the student body ideals of honesty, sincerity, earnestness, tolerance, and social and political obligations." The University Committee on the Kemper K. Knapp Bequest, in addition to setting up the Knapp Scholarships and Fellowships, has sponsored from time to time lectures, conferences, and visiting professorships in the belief that extracurricular lectures on appropriate subjects by outstanding men representing various points of view would appeal to the imagination of our students and might help to awaken in the student body a sharper understanding of the privileges and responsibilities which as citizens of this country and the world we have all inherited.

The lectures here published were delivered by Professor Edward C. Kirkland of Bowdoin College in the course of the second semester of the academic year 1950–51 when he was Kemper K. Knapp Visiting Professor of History in the University of Wisconsin.

PREFACE

IT HAS long been my conviction that lectures should not be written to be printed but should be designed as an attempt at oral communication with an audience. In this spirit the three lectures in this volume were delivered to the customary audience on a university or college campus; one composed of faculty colleagues, graduate students, undergraduates, and envoys from the world outside the academic community. They are reprinted exactly as they were given. For me, nonetheless, they are something more than a souvenir of a happy occasion. I hope they will serve as a first step in the revaluation I am undertaking of the period between the Civil War and the beginning of the twentieth century. I am, of course, deeply grateful to the Knapp Committee, to the members of the History Department, and to others who made possible the delivery of these lectures.

Edward C. Kirkland

Brunswick, Maine

CONTENTS

BUSINESS IN THE GILDED AGE

–I–

THE BUREAUCRAT LOOKS
AT THE BUSINESSMAN

The first act is to set the stage. Our time is the period between the Civil War and the twentieth century, a period when the United States became the greatest industrial nation of the world. By the dull statistics commonly used to measure such achievements, she wrested the historic leadership in such matters from Great Britain and outraced the contemporary rivalry of Germany. Our dramatis personae are the business leaders of that generation: John D. Rockefeller, the "oil king"; Andrew Carnegie, the "star-spangled Scotchman," steel-maker and bestower of libraries and teachers' pensions; Commodore Vanderbilt, a steamboater who made a fortune in his old age from the New York Central and other railroads; Daniel Drew, like Vanderbilt a steamboat man and later the power behind the Erie Railroad; James J. Hill, who forced the Great Northern Railroad from the Mississippi to the Pacific and won the cognomen of the "Empire Builder"; J. P. Morgan, "Jupiter" Morgan, practically a synonym for the hated Wall Street; and C. P. Huntington and Leland Stanford, whose fortunes won on transcontinental and other railroads gave a cultural patina to California.

Naturally the performers thought well of their play and of themselves. John D. Rockefeller summarized his motives and his harassed career, "I had no ambition to make a fortune. Mere money-getting has never been my goal. I saw a marvelous future for our country, and I wanted to participate in the work of making our country great. I had an ambition to build."[1] But the critics were loath to accept this favorable verdict as true or final. If they were reformers, they detected at work the "old self interest," and in large measure identified the business practices of the era with sin. Though the historians have brought a more balanced judgment, they have used in general a subdued palette and were prone to picture the twentieth century of Woodrow Wilson and the two Roosevelts as a time when America struggled out of the darkness into light. The period here under survey has become "The Gilded Age." The title suggests its false and meretricious character. The business leaders were "robber barons." Though this derogation frequently lacked precise definition, it suggests an unwholesome lust for riches and their acquisition through the levying of tribute rather than through honest toil. It is the purpose of these three essays not necessarily to upset this valuation but to bring to bear upon it the judgments of three conservative critics in a position to be acquainted at firsthand with the business phenomena of this extraordinary era. Though the approach will be an individual one, I shall, as far as feasibility permits,

1. J. T. Flynn, *God's Gold: The Story of Rockefeller and His Times* (New York: Harcourt Brace & Company, 1940), p. 201.

regard the individual critic as representing a somewhat more generalized approach.

As IN ALL beginnings, it is appropriate to begin with an Adams. Charles Francis Adams, Jr., was the great-grand-son of one president, the grandson of another, the son of Charles Francis Adams, American minister to Great Britain during the American Civil War, and the brother of Henry Adams, whose intellectual pilgrimages and speculations have formed almost a cult. On his graduation from Harvard, where his education, like that of his brother Henry, was largely a "failure," Charles studied in a desultory fashion for the law and was admitted to the bar largely, by his own confession, because the examiner knew the family and hoped the character of the young man would overcome his legal ignorance. Then the Civil War caught him up, he became the white colonel of a Negro regiment. The war was his education. A half-century of full activity followed. At one time or another he was manager and custodian of a considerable family fortune, a gifted amateur historian, overseer of Harvard University for nearly a quarter of a century, President of the Union Pacific Railroad, and so successfully active in the affairs of the family town, Quincy, and of Massachusetts that he could write in his autobiography "*This*, I did" for a public library, a reformation of the town schools which attracted national attention, and a park system which saved for metropolitan Boston some of its irreplaceable physical attractions like the Blue Hills and the Middlesex Fells.

For our purposes he was a bureaucrat. He served on the railroad commission of Massachusetts in the pioneer ten years after its creation in 1869. For a large share of this decade he was its chairman; he was always its dominating figure. When he resigned in 1879, he became chairman of the Board of Arbitrators established by the railroads in the trunk-line territory, the Northeast and Midwest, to settle their disputes. This position he held for three years. Though it was private employment, its nature made it bureaucratic. Characteristically Adams played this role convinced it was futile. Bureaucracy, he announced, was a natural growth in northern Prussia; it was hostile to the American genius. In a diagnosis which would later have delighted the National Association of Manufacturers, he derided the weaknesses of commissions, the American form of bureaus. "As a rule," he declared, "they do not work well. Not only do they develop in too many cases a singular aptitude for all jobbery, but even when honestly composed, they rarely accomplish much. Once created, also, they can never be gotten rid of. They ever after remain part of the machinery of government, drawing salaries and apparently making work for themselves to do."[2] With a contrariness equally characteristic, Adams made himself a specialist in railroad matters, so he could make commissions operate with effectiveness, and he felt his appointment to the Massachusetts Commission placed him in his proper niche.

2. Charles Francis Adams, Jr., *Railroads: Their Origin and Problems* (New York: G. P. Putman's Sons, 1893), p. 132.

As bureaucratic critic of his business generation, Adams presents difficulties. Some of them are inherent in the selection of any individual for that purpose. Even the ideas of the most principled or recalcitrant change over the years and the judgments of age are not the judgments of youth. We will confront this discontinuity in Adams. A personal preference for paradoxical utterance, for reversing his field, for startling reader and hearer heightened his inconsistencies. In the seventies he could labor like a Moses to lead the Massachusetts railroads to adopt a standard and improved system of keeping their business accounts and in this field, lecture railroad executives on detail and policy with all the dogmatism of a complete revelation from Mount Sinai. A decade later he could inform a Congressional investigating committee that "I am not a book-keeper or an expert in book-keeping. . . . When it comes to going to the books themselves and examining them in detail, I could not understand them if I did, I do not know enough of book-keeping to enable me to go into them intelligently. It is a foreign language to me."[3] These occasions, on both of which he was equally candid, illustrate the "other-mindedness" which Adams realized was his outstanding intellectual characteristic.

It is a limitation, too, that his expert observation was largely confined to the railroads. This is, however, a small defect. In the years under discussion the railroads were the most advanced and conspicuous of business enterprises. The panics of these years were railroad

3. Fiftieth Cong., 1 sess., Sen. Exec. Doc. 51, *Testimony*, p. 89.

panics. Nor, since he was not a textbook writer or professor, did he ever systematize his thought into a harmonious whole. The reacher for Adams' opinions must resort, therefore, to his famous dissection of the Erie Railroad, *A Chapter of Erie,* written while he was making his reputation as a railroad expert, to other essays in the same period of the late sixties, to the reports of the Massachusetts Railroad Commission which the other less literate members of that body always permitted him to write, to testimony which he gave before Congressional committees, and to an autobiography deservedly less famous than the *Education* of his brother. But these random expressions of attitudes have the supreme advantage of stemming from experience and occasion. His judgments were informed. They were also highly individual. Any young officer who repeated during the dusty days of Gettysburg, lines from Milton's *Samson Agonistes* will not be commonplace.

The most cursory reading of Adams' essays, reports, and testimony reveals a recurrent theme. He wrote constantly of returning to fundamental principles, correct principles, first causes. There is many a reference to law, including the "great force of natural law," and sometimes to the "laws of sound economy." These are often given greater explicitness. Luckily, I have found only one reference to that darling of the platitude utterer, "the law of supply and demand." Somewhat more frequent is the reference to "the law of self-preservation" and "the law of the survival of the fittest." But he reserves his deepest obeisance for the law of combination:

"where combination was possible, competition was impossible."[4] In turn this was but one aspect of a greater law, the "law of gravitation." At one and the same time this inclusive generalization creates business consolidations, draws commerce and industry into great cities, and sends the countryside into decline. Although these laws are often spoken of as "irresistible" and their violation as "folly," it is clear that Adams thought them more relative than absolute. There is, for one thing, a gradation in their certainty. Geographical laws are comparatively inexorable; political laws more subject to voluntary manipulation. Moreover most laws are constantly upset by "surprises." Nor are the laws or first principles of universal application. They depend on locality, the level of economic development, differences in national outlook, and variations in taste. Nor were they a juggernaut rolling over the individual. In the impish essays in which he sought both secret and cure for Boston's economic decline, Adams suddenly found he was caught by a predestination in which he did not thoroughly believe. The energy, daring, and intelligence of individuals and communities could within limits modify forces and laws. These last two, ever changing, must be constantly rediscovered and restated.

From his *Autobiography*, where Adams constantly reveals the care with which he planned his life, it is clear that this preference for law and principle is at its simplest a Puritan preference for prudence and fore-

4. Adams, "Railroad Inflation," *North American Review*, CVIII, 150.

thought. It was something more. A reading of John Stuart Mill's essay on Auguste Comte "revolutionized in a single morning my whole mental attitude. I emerged from the theological stage, in which I had been nurtured, and passed into the scientific."[5] He went on to read Darwin. In short, the current concern with science helped build the Adams' structure of thought. Like his own inheritance, it made him impatient with "chance," "anarchy," "chaos," words constantly at the end of his pen. He sought knowledge, factual knowledge. The essential weapon in that search was "observation." While Darwin through observation "rewrote Genesis," the Harvard of Adams' time clung to the humanities and theology, and thought "the intelligent use of the eyes was beneath its dignity, and none of its affair."[6] Observation requires access to materials. Adams had, therefore, an apostolic belief in publicity. Whether working for more accurate statistics of railroad mileage, a system of railroad accounts comprehensible to the examiner and investor, or condemning the Central Pacific because a small clique in California veiled its internal arrangements in "about the same obscurity as are the rites of Freemasonry,"[7] Adams was bent upon dispelling "mystery" and seeing things as they were. Without unimpeded observation and the resultant knowledge, the

5. Adams, *An Autobiography* (Boston: Houghton Mifflin Company, 1916), p. 179.

6. Adams, *Three Phi Beta Kappa Addresses* (Boston: Houghton Mifflin Company, 1907), pp. 120, 127.

7. Adams, "Railroad Inflation," *North American Review,* CVIII, 147.

"sweet order" for which Adams always called was impossible. These, it should be pointed out, were essentially the objectives of the bureaucrat. He cannot administer chaos; he can only direct a system. If he dared hope for anything from government commissions, it was because they might bring to bear upon practical affairs the tools of investigation and thus formulate a science and a system.

The contemporary business world was far from conforming to the Adams prescription of what should be. If it had any system, it was a system of flux. There were few elements of permanence or of stable adjustment. Instead, all was "ugly change" and "violent fluctuations" without the ordered and logical sequences Adams so admired. In short, it was the era of competition. This passionate strife had something to recommend it; it spurred men to rivalry and made them accomplish the impossible. But its final effects upon the business system and upon businessmen were deteriorating. Gripped in the inexorability of the competitive order, the lesser businessmen, "men of routine" as Adams called them, developed "the quality known as 'smartness,' which with them verged usually on a low cunning. As a rule, their highest ambition was to get 'their share of the business,' and in doing so they were quite indifferent about destroying its value. Capable, energetic, bustling, and with no faith in each other, they made agreements which they neither expected would be kept, nor intended themselves to keep, and, when not deceiving others, were anxiously watching to see that they were not deceived themselves."[8] "Honor for its own sake and good faith apart from self-interest are, in a business point of view, symptoms of youth and defective education."[9] At other times, it was not so much the smartness, cunning, and dishonesty of officials and agents that impressed Adams as their indolence, inertia, and stupidity. They preferred to do a small business at a large profit rather than a large one at a small because the latter involved more energy and a "sacrifice of ease." They so dragged their feet when innovations of technology or of business methods were proposed that Adams meditated a figurative resort to the whipping post. "Nothing but this appeal . . . seems to produce the needed mental activity; for it is difficult to realize the stupid conservatism of ordinary men when brought to the consideration of something to which they are not accustomed."[10]

Of the men in the higher echelons of business, Adams had opportunity for observation. In his *Autobiography* he wrote, "I have known, and known tolerably well, a good many 'successful' men—'big' financially—men famous during the last half-century."[11] To compare them with the barons of the Middle Ages was a "grotesque absurdity." They might be vulgar; but they had ability. At the very end of the sixties, Adams in *A Chapter of Erie* pictured Vanderbilt as under the pall of playing

8. *Tenth Annual Report of the* [Mass.] *Board of Railroad Commissioners, 1879,* p. 56.

9. Adams, *Railroads: Their Origin and Problems,* p. 194.

10. Adams, *Notes on Railroad Accidents* (New York: G. P. Putnam's Sons, 1879), pp. 64–65.

11. Adams, *An Autobiography,* p. 190.

whist and loving horseflesh, selfish, hard, unscrupulous, and ambitious. Still, he was a man of large ideas. Though he operated by instinct rather than intellectual effort, he understood the railroad system and by the "law of gravitation and centralization" moved to become its despot. This process then filled Adams with admiration and apprehension. Less than a decade later the apprehension had changed to approval. To stop the competitive railroad wars then raging required a Caesar or a Napoleon. "If the elder Vanderbilt were alive and in the full possession of his power, he probably would solve the difficulty in the way most natural to him."[12] Luckily his descendants had continued his task, working with the fundamental law almost unconsciously sensed by the founder of the dynasty.

Adams indicted big business men not because they were incompetent but because "I am more than a little puzzled to account for the instances I have seen of business success—money-getting. It comes from a rather low instinct. Certainly, so far as my observation goes, it is rarely met with in combination with the finer or more interesting traits of character. . . . A less interesting crowd I do not care to encounter. Not one that I have ever known would I care to meet again, either in this world or the next. . . . A set of mere money-getters and traders, they were essentially unattractive and uninteresting."[13] His experience with the Union Pacific directors led him to repeat the indictment. "They were

12. Adams, *Railroads: Their Origin and Problems*, p. 195.
13. Adams, *An Autobiography*, p. 190.

a coarse, realistic, bargaining crowd,"[14] he observed.

This attack upon money-getting did not stem from a mere dislike for economic achievements. Adams frequently employed his vigorous vocabulary to celebrate materialism of this sort. Fulton's invention of the steamboat, the industrial diversity of Massachusetts, the reduction of railroad rates on grain from the West—all these reduced him to awe and wonder. In the course of discussing the old theory of railroad managers that locomotive engineers should stand on unsheltered platforms lest they become careless and go to sleep, he sounded a delightful grace note on the benefits of materialism: "It took years in Great Britain for intelligent railroad managers to learn that the more protected and comfortable a man is the better he will attend to his duty."[15] Nor did the attack upon money-getting imply an attack upon profits. Far from questioning them, Adams regarded profits as essential. He spoke approvingly of the "deep self-interest" of the businessman. Though he did not bother to attach the dignity of law, natural or economic, to the observation, he asserted, "Every one knows that self-interest is necessary to the wise and economical management of all property."[16] Profits were necessary also to induce investment. A missionary for the correct use of general statistics, he refused to be alarmed by individual instances of generous returns. Though he found plenty to censure in the manner in which the first

14. *Ibid.*, p. 195.
15. Adams, *Railroad Accidents*, p. 179.
16. Adams, "The Railroad System," *North American Review*, CIV, 508.

transcontinental railroads, the Union and Central Pacific, were thrust in the sixties across the West, the level of returns to their promoters and builders was not one of them. "Those who took its construction in hand incurred great risk, and at one time trembled on the verge of ruin. This enterprise was to them a lottery, in which they might well draw a blank, but should they draw a prize, the greatness of the prize must justify the risk incurred."[17]

Where business was concerned, Adams condemned money-getting for the methods employed to get money. Not so much the goal but the procedure unloosed his thunderbolts of satiric disapproval. Piracy, no longer found on the high seas, was domesticated on land; it invaded business and enabled adventurers to harm the public on a new scale. "Gambling is a business now where formerly it was a disreputable excitement. Cheating at cards was always disgraceful; transactions of a similar character under the euphemistic names of 'operating,' 'cornering,' and the like are not so regarded."[18] By creating paper stock and inventing capital, men grew rich without hard labor and by a sleight of hand concealed a "swindle." Directors speculated in the stock of their own companies, manipulated the market, and betrayed the welfare of their wards, the other stockholders. While Adams might grudgingly admire Vanderbilt, he had nothing but contempt for the latter's New York

17. Adams, "Railroad Inflation," *North American Review,* CVIII, 145.

18. C. F. Adams, Jr. and Henry Adams, *Chapters of Erie and Other Essays* (New York: Henry Holt & Company, 1886), p. 2.

rival, Daniel Drew of the Erie Railroad. This "Speculative Director" was "shrewd, unscupulous, and very illiterate—a strange combination of superstition and faithlessness," less to be tolerated than the ordinary gambler since he combined "the character of the traitor with the acts of the thief."[19]

In the conduct of their business, railroads gave rebates to individual shippers, passes to those with influence, and discriminations to certain shipping points—all forms of favor and of privilege. Entering agreements only with the expectation of breaking them, railroad men had neither honor nor good faith. Quite heedless of the old truth that you could not serve two masters, they mingled the affairs of the company with their own for the continued benefit of themselves. "They receive money into one hand as a corporation, and pay it into the other as a contractor. Humanly speaking, the whole thing seems to be a species of thimble-rig, with this difference from the ordinary arrangement, that whereas commonly 'the little joker' is never found under the thimble which may be turned up, in this case he is sure to be found, turn up which thimble one may."[20] Extravagance, fraud, dishonesty, and recklessness were at every hand.

Even the pure in heart, even an Adams who believed in order and system could not escape contamination. Such was the lesson of his experience as President of the

19. *Ibid.*, pp. 5, 8.
20. Adams, "Railroad Inflation," *North American Review,* CVIII, 148.

Union Pacific in the eighties. Adams had early sensed the danger. There seem to be "peculiarly demoralizing influences about the position of a railroad official," he wrote in his article on Boston; and surveying the building Pacific Railroad he prophesied that it would be the richest and most powerful corporation in the world and probably "the most corrupt." Now Adams was there. The contrast of his practice with his past preachment was painful. Though he had never paralleled his brother Henry's sharp abuse of Jay Gould, a broker, gambler, and "spider" of intrigue, he had described his depredations with exactitude. Now Adams was of the opinion that Gould, an associate on the Union Pacific, had grown more responsible with age and was working for the benefit of the railroad rather than his pocket. Some scholars incline to this view, it has yet to be demonstrated. That great evil, personal rebates, which he had once condemned, Adams reluctantly authorized as essential to keeping the competitive business. Once the high priest of pitiless publicity, Adams was now the apologist for concealment. "It is no use for me to slaughter the interests of the company intrusted to my hands. If I am playing a game of chance, and I show my hand where nobody else engaged in the game does, the effect is not long to be waited for."[21] In sum, Adams asserted he was not a railroad reformer. "I am an official of a corporation."[22]

21. Fiftieth Cong., 1 sess., Sen. Exec. Doc. 51, *Testimony*, p. 1999.
22. *Ibid.*, p. 96.

Rather than smirking, as some contemporaries and successors have done, over this downfall of the visionary, who, Adams had repeatedly asserted, was more practical than practical men, it is more illuminating to examine the dilemma of the man of order and science in an era of competition. There were moments when Adams wrote as if knowledge were everything, and that it would conquer of its own power. He suspected force. With it he was wont to couple the adjective "ignorant." As he said of the Granger railroad commissions of the Midwest, "They were where they were, not to study a difficult problem and to guide their steps by the light of investigation. Nothing of this sort was, as a rule, expected of them. On the contrary they were there to prosecute. ... In a word they represented force. That under these circumstances they succeeded at all is the true cause of astonishment."[23] But Adams' own experience as railroad commissioner and as arbitrator of the trunk lines convinced him that more than the good faith of railroad men and the rationality of their decisions was required to make them obey agreements they had signed. "They need constantly to feel that a policeman's eye is upon them, and that there is a station house in the next street."[24] In short force was necessary. At the moment Adams preferred that businessmen organize to apply it.

Another choice would have been the intervention of the government, an alternative Adams saw as inevitable

23. Adams, *Railroads: Their Origin and Problems,* p. 135.
24. *Ibid.,* p. 193.

if monopoly ruled the business world. But the prospect of force exerted by the government filled him with far more dismay than force in the hands of individuals. Salvation by the government was an *ignis fatuus*. Government was ignorant of business. Its intervention into affairs of management was meddlesome and cumbersome. It could not master intricate economical laws. It was absurd to talk about knowledge in a legislature; few individual legislators served long enough to acquire it concerning the affairs which came within their jurisdiction. The financier would always get ahead of the lawmaker. These objections to governmental force were not theoretical. They sprang from Adams' faculty of concrete observation. *A Chapter of Erie* is not alone an acid portrayal of business wrongdoing. It is a picture of befuddled and venal judges and of legislators bought in job lots by Jay Gould and Commodore Vanderbilt or their representatives. If the railroad commission were an escape from both corruption and stupidity, it was only when it lacked "force," only when it was a species of lens focusing the rays of public opinion upon abuses.

Nor was Adams sure about public opinion. An examination of an uninstructed people was certainly far from reassuring. Their spokesmen employed not the language of scientific analysis, but the "bathos of extravagance" or the demagoguery of "robber barons," "bloated bondholders," and "money sharks." To such cant a large class were willing victims and the power of words and phrases over the popular mind prevented argument or refutation. People felt and did not reason. Impatient, they were unwilling to wait for calm science to work itself out; the man in the street wanted to get things done and disposed of. Granted the people were honest, they were still careless, indifferent, and superficial. "They are apt to believe what they are pleased to call the evidence of their own senses, than which no evidence can be more deceptive. . . . They hug their heavy burdens, being only wise in their own conceit."[25] Indeed a "diseased public opinion" admired the standards of business practice which Adams condemned.

The real tragedy of Adams was that he had nowhere to turn. The business leaders were a damned generation. The "Dear Peepul" of his *Autobiography* were little better. Persuasion and force, force or persuasion—all were vanities. In despair he sorrowfully committed the society to which he had given so much thought and energy to the grimmest of all laws, "the survivalship of the fittest." This surrender was more than the disillusionment of a bureaucrat; it was a personal tragedy.

25. Adams, "Railroad Inflation," *North American Review*, CVIII, 132, 134.

–II–

THE MORALIST LOOKS
AT THE BUSINESSMAN

In November 1856, on the eve of a presidential election, Edwin Lawrence Godkin arrived from Europe in New York. The young man, just twenty-five, aspired to become an American lawyer. He was certainly a distinctive immigrant. Though born in Ireland, he did not conform to the pattern of Irish immigration currently descending on America's shores. Rather, his family was English and his father a Presbyterian minister of parts. Godkin's own career as Crimean War correspondent and journalist removed him from the ranks of the starving or needy; precociously successful, he had already written a history of Hungary and the Magyars. His biographer implies he was drawn to America by an enthusiasm for America's democratic experiment. It is not impossible. It seems just as likely that the British system of a caste society and of political and economic privilege drove Godkin hither. Years later in an attack on the alleged superiority of aristocratic government, he wrote with obvious personal feeling that the English government "treats dissent as a crime, and punishes it by civil and social disability, and makes the most honest callings a ground of social disgrace and discredit."[1]

Within a decade after his arrival in the United States, this dissenter, armed as he was with letters of introduction to the learned and influential, had entered the American bar, performed chores for an English commercial house in the South, served as correspondent for the London *Daily News*, married into a New Haven family of culture and wealth, and with the aid of American friends, the most influential of whom were from Cambridge, raised a capital of $100,000 to found a weekly journal, *The Nation*. It resembled its modern successor only in its independence. In 1881 Henry Villard, a German immigrant and one of the most successful business giants of his day—he completed the Northern Pacific Railroad—purchased the New York *Post* and with exemplary forbearance entrusted the formulation and statement of policy to the editors. Of these Godkin soon became the chief. The *Nation* also underwent a transformation, it became the weekly edition of the *Post*. Though now an anthology of selected daily editorials, the *Nation* was still Godkin.

On his retirement in 1900, as on many earlier occasions, the discriminating saluted Godkin's immense editorial influence. Like the New York *World*, his was a newspaperman's publication. Editors and reporters waited for his opinion. Like the Mencken *Mercury* of the nineteen-twenties, a comparison which I am sure would make Godkin shudder, the *Nation* was the jour-

1. E. L. Godkin, "The Tyranny of the Majority," *North American Review*, CIV, 226.

nal of the young college generation. From philosophers like William James, educators like Charles W. Eliot, publicists like Viscount Bryce, came letters of deep approval. For Godkin introduced something new into the American journalism of his day. The great persuaders, he was convinced, were the pulpit and the press. The former had lost its influence; the latter had become too personal, partisan, and passionate. So he wedded the two callings into the prophet-publicist. He intended that the *Nation* should be dedicated and remotely Olympian. "If journalism," he wrote, "is to play the part in democracy to which it aspires," the journalist must be anonymous, surrender the hope of political office, and seek only to extend his influence and his ideas. He must "become, in short, a Voice, and nothing more."[2] It was the role of the "Voice," he printed it with the upper case V, that Godkin fulfilled.

For judging contemporary businessmen and business methods, this exalted role had limitations. Too often Godkin substituted theoretical generalizations for concrete opinions based upon an examination of contemporary actuality. While Charles Francis Adams was skirting the libel laws in his "A Chapter of Erie" in the *North American Review,* Godkin was writing for the same magazine abstractions about democracy. Years later, Charles W. Eliot, in a typical Cantabrigian letter intended to be complimentary to Godkin, noted the same defect. Such generalizations, repeated as editors have to repeat them, easily became hackneyed and con-

2. Godkin, "The Democratic View of Democracy," *North American Review,* CI, 133.

ventional. A steady reading of the *Nation* during the Godkin era can produce surfeit. Nonetheless the editor had the saving grace of style. A foe of cant, he had a keen eye for fallacies and a swift way with humbug. If not humorous, he was witty, occasionally at his own expense. In the highest sense of the word, he brought learning to his task. He was well read in economics, politics, history. Literature and biography were his delights. This erudition, coupled with his European background, made it certain that the American scene would be given perspective.

Though his background was so varied, it is not too great a simplification to see in Godkin a Thomas Jefferson translated to the second half of the nineteenth century. Like Jefferson, the former distrusted the wealth and misery of cities. Of the agricultural life and of the farmer, he wrote a panegyric that the master of Monticello might have envied. In his conception of education and aristocracy and their role in society and government service, he was in the same tradition. Though, like all editors who are compelled to meet deadlines and have opinions on daily events, Godkin had neither the memory nor the time to be consistent and, like all thoughtful individuals, changed his mind with experience and age, he never wavered on freedom. In 1870 he began an article for the *North American Review* with the assertion that in the whole literature of politics there was "no nobler word" than "liberty."[3] Nearly a quarter of a century later as he scolded the rich for their idle-

3. Godkin, "The Prospects of the Political Art," *North American Review*, CX, 398.

ness, a vice he found intolerable, he added, "The best thing in the world is individual freedom. . . . Better that ten men should loaf than that one should lose his liberty."[4]

On the whole Godkin looked with more complacence than Adams upon the economic advance of the United States, upon the goal of money-getting, and, with limitations, upon the way fortunes were acquired. His scrutiny both of American history and contemporary America convinced him that such materialism was inevitable. He might as well accept it. His analysis was an exceptionally shrewd one. The materialism of the United States, and incidentally its keen individualism and democratic equality, was due originally to its newness and its colonial status. After the American Revolution, the westward movement perpetuated and intensified these conditions and exalted the practical qualities which enabled native Americans and immigrants to solve the unique problems of new lands. The whole development, proceeding first at steamboat and then at railroad speed, inevitably brought a devotion to material pursuits, "necessary at the outset," and now "made absorbing in a country like the West, by the richness of the prizes which are offered to shrewd speculation and successful industry. Where possible or even probable gains are so great, the whole community gives itself up to the chase of them with an eagerness which is not democratic, but human."[5] In short, almost thirty years

4. Godkin, "Idleness and Immorality," *Forum*, XIII, 341.

5. Godkin, "Aristocratic Opinions of Democracy," *North American Review*, C, 209–219.

before Frederick Jackson Turner's famous essay on the "Significance of the Frontier in American History," Godkin was writing about the qualities of the "Western Man," and he was isolating "the frontier life" as a unique influence upon American political, social, and economic institutions. He mustered in behalf of this theory an eloquence the equal of Turner's and anticipated to an extraordinary degree much of the latter's detailed assertions and methodology. He utilized the comparative method. An examination, for example, of the Australian frontier, reinforced Godkin's conclusions about the American phenomenon. He even stated the safety-valve theory. The fact that they had the "Prairies at their back" made the American laboring men independent, restless, and able to secure higher wages.

Though the West may have been the most American explanation for an inevitable American materialism, it was not the only one. In the older parts of the nation, science was making possible an amplitude of production hitherto undreamed of. Steam power, steam locomotion, the electric telegraph, and the electric cable coupled with a generosity of natural resources and a great market area, to which Americans had foresightedly applied the doctrines of free trade, stimulated commercial ambition and business cupidity on a scale before unmatched. On the whole this great productivity was to the good. Production, though it might heap up great fortunes certain to corrupt, if not their makers, at least those who inherited them, solved problems, more particularly the labor problem. Over this question Godkin worried for decades in statements generally more remarkable for their tone of reprimand and irritation than for insight. The labor problem, he finally concluded, was in essence the problem of keeping the manual laborers contented. Perhaps it was insoluble. Labor will always reproduce and press on the means of subsistence, and thus its lot will always be one of want and woe. Still, abundant material satisfactions might postpone the evil day. "Physical comfort among the great bulk of mankind tends to produce happiness."[6] Without production the nation could not eliminate poverty.

The concept of law buttressed Godkin's indulgent estimate of American business advance. By law he did not mean statutes, but that array of fundamental and first principles which had also fascinated Adams. Both science and history contributed to a knowledge of these laws. Though by the late seventies he was writing in the *Nation* of the survival of the fittest, he revealed the possibility of deriving this concept from other sources than Darwinism. "The great law which nature seems to have prescribed for the government of the world, and the only law of human society which we are able to extract from history, is that the more intelligent and thoughtful of the race shall inherit the earth and have the best time, and that all others shall find life on the whole dull and unprofitable. Socialism is an attempt to contravene this law, and ensure a good time to everybody independently of character and talents."[7] Of equal

6. Godkin, "The Economic Man," *North American Review,* CLIII, 499–500.

7. Godkin, "Duty of Educated Men in a Democracy," *Forum,* XVII, 43–44.

stature and dignity were the laws of economics, derived from human nature. Human nature was a constant, in all times and lands. So America, whatever American politicians and demagogues might assert, was governed by the same economical laws as Europe, perhaps more so because here they had freer play.

Over these economic laws Godkin sometimes cast an air of relativeness. The educational, social, and political milieu hampered or frustrated their operation. Indeed observation sometimes revealed that the ideal formulations of political economy did not accord with reality. Once in an unguarded moment he so far slipped from the true faith as to deny that the labor bargain between an individual worker and the employer was either free or what the economists said it was. What the laborer agrees to do under the duress of getting a job, "I agree to do under compulsion, just as much as if I agreed to do it with a pistol at my head; and the terms I make under such circumstances are not by any means the measure of my rights, even 'under the laws of trade.' When, therefore, political economists talk of wages as being fixed by the proportion which labor bears to capital at any given time and place, they presuppose a state of things which is purely ideal."[8] In later years Godkin drifted away from such heresies and back to a firmer belief in the laws formulated by the classical economists, Ricardo, Malthus, Adam Smith, John Stuart Mill, and Richard Cobden. In accordance with the laws of eco-

8. Godkin, "The Labor Crisis," *North American Review*, CV, 185–186.

nomic individualism and of competition between individuals, producers sought to sell in the dearest market and buy in the cheapest, employers sought to buy their labor for the lowest wages, and workers gave the least labor for the wages they received. Whether this universal selfishness and struggle worked out for good, Godkin did not say directly. It was enough for him that the science of political economy "is based on the assumption that men are free and independent."[9]

Though a believer in historical conditioning and in the laws of trade might conceivably shrug off the knaveries of the most predatory businessman as inherent in the nature of things, Godkin was a world away from this Nirvana of tired sophistication. For the mainspring of his thought and conviction was morality. The evidence is overwhelming. Within a week after his arrival in the United States, he noted with delight that the questions of slavery and related issues "were half moral and only half political or legal."[10] In the tradition of his intellectual masters, he was the foe of protection. While often willing to discuss this issue on the basis of expediency or of "the natural law of human intercourse,"[11] the moral argument really set his zeal afire. Thus Cobden's great virtue was "his full apprehension of the moral bearings"[12] of free trade, and in a typical state-

9. Godkin, "Aristocratic Opinions of Democracy," North American Review, C, 226.
10. Rollo Ogden, ed., Life and Letters of Edwin Lawrence Godkin (New York: The Macmillan Company, 1907), I, 112.
11. "The Revision of the Tariff," Nation, VIII, 44.
12. "Cobden," Nation, XXVI, 13.

ment of his own position Godkin declared the protective tariff amassed "a corruption fund. By this I do not mean a fund distributed in bribes ... but a fund the existence of which must be constantly present to the mind of the lazy, the improvident, or incompetent. . . . That such a system could long prevail in any country without damage to the moral constitution of those who were benefited by it, all experience of human nature forbids us to expect."[13] Viscount Bryce, long his friend, correspondent, and admirer, wrote as the epitaph on Godkin's tombstone that he was "Publicist, Economist, Moralist."[14]

Only in a residual way was Godkin's morality of divine sanction. An Episcopalian, perhaps because his wife was or perhaps because it was the most latitudinarian of faiths, he was no formal Christian. On this point he was quite explicit. If Milan cathedral almost persuaded him to be a Christian, the contemplation of contemporary Christianity soon repelled him. Catholicism hampered the freedom of speculation. Protestantism had dropped the old sanctions of heaven and hell which kept the multitudes moral and had substituted "a gospel of social endeavour" for the old Calvinistic theology which at least inculcated certain conceptions of duty as you cut your eye teeth on it. Ethical ministers, for whom Godkin had a scarcely concealed disdain, were more concerned with humanity than honesty. Still

13. Godkin, "Some Political and Social Aspects of the Tariff," *New Princeton Review*, III, 165, 167.
14. Ogden, *op. cit.*, II, 256.

Godkin was not entirely able to keep a sort of God out of affairs. Since somebody had to create human nature, the constant which underlay law, it is not entirely surprising to learn that "the principle of competition... is the law by which Providence secures the progress of the human race. It is not a law of political economy simply; it is a law of human nature, and the folly of the Communists and Socialists has consisted in the delusion that they could get rid of this law."[15]

Much more frequent in Godkin's writing is the notion that morality grows out of the historical process and is a rationalization and justification for the historical event. This theory, I am tempted to surmise, was peculiarly serviceable in controversies when the editor desired to shatter the pompous infallibilities of arguments and contestants he disliked. But it was more than a debater's weapon. When those who possessed "brute power" or the "knowledge which dominates brute power" became the "first capitalists, and naturally assumed the task of superintendence" and the weak and ignorant became laborers, "as is usual, a code of morality was framed to support this doctrine."[16] Elsewhere in an admirable essay he discusses at length the evolution of the qualities or virtues of the ideal merchant. That he should adopt this approach at all is illuminating. That he

15. Godkin, "Cooperation," *North American Review*, CVI, 173; "The Economic Man," *North American Review*, CLIII, 502; "The Democratic View of Democracy," *North American Review*, CI, 109.
16. Godkin, "Cooperation," *North American Review*, CVI, 153.

should without regret conclude that the modern man of business need not work his way up by frugality, industry, punctuality, and integrity "and that the decline of these virtues, considered simply as commercial instruments, and not as moral qualities, has a good foundation in reason,"[17] is even more surprising.

Then just as Godkin, as in this instance, seems about to formulate codes of business conduct based on his genuine ability at observation and analysis, he comes back to that "conscience" whose existence, in spite of the scientific skepticism over its exact localization in the human organism, is demonstrated by the results of its operation. The morality of the Presbyterian manse overwhelms him and his thought stands once more in the shadow of the awesome absolutes: sobriety, thrift, discipline, honesty, and effort. It is in this mood that he unrolls the far too simple syllogism: The modern economy depends on credit, credit depends on promises, promises depend on faith and honesty. It is in this temper that he constantly reminds supporters of the silver currency and greenbacks, and the tinkerers with the public debt that they are in fact advocating a swindle, a fraud, and a cheat. These moral standards explain his preference for agriculture over manufacturing. He doubted if American manufacturing can ever produce as successfully as agriculture "that stern, simple, enduring, self-reliant, self-respecting type of character which must, after all, form the basis of any nation which seeks

17. Godkin, "Commercial Immorality and Political Corruption," *North American Review*, CVII, 249–250.

to do great things, or leave a shining mark in history."[18]
Still these embattled virtues were more pleasant if
spiced with sophistication. As Godkin wrote of a Con-
gressman from Massachusetts, "Dawes seemed a *good*
man, with whom life had gone hard, but who tried to
do his duty. One gets sick of this class, however."[19]

Thus equipped, Godkin was bound to censure much
of what he saw in business and the businessmen of the
Gilded Age. In a magazine article, appropriately en-
titled "Commercial Immorality," he condemned the
business methods just after the Civil War as reckless ⊢
and dishonest, and in the columns of the *Nation* blazed
out against the indifference of railroad officials to the
loss of life on their lines and their jobbery in the construction and management of railroads. Even Wall
Street was "in many respects an odious demon." Such
corruption was worse when its contamination spread
from the field of mere money-making into politics. As
a matter of course, American capitalists asserted their
ability to purchase venal legislators and other officials.

Sometimes the deeper changes in American business,
the concentration of wealth, and the dependence of the
mass of Americans upon supercapitalists, dismayed him.
From "the morass of reckless extravagance, of paper
money and national debt, of public and private corruption," grew Fisk and Vanderbilt, "twin colossi of wealth
and power, who . . . dispose with more than imperial

18. Godkin, "The Labor Crisis," *North American Review,* CV,
205.
19. Ogden, *op. cit.,* I, 311.

despotism of the lives, liberties and property of a large portion of their fellow citizens. . . ."[20] More dangerous than individuals were the large corporations with their swollen treasuries and anonymity. Voicing suspicions hardly different from those held by the Grangers, whom he usually identified with communists, Godkin condemned corporate potentialities for financial skulduggery; the unscrupulousness of organizations that could not have consciences; the presence of huge slush funds; and the power over armies of employees. "Corporations are as powerful as individual noblemen or aristocrats were in England in the last century, or in France before the Revolution, but are far harder to get at or to bring to justice, from their habit of making terms with their enemies instead of fighting them."[21]

To redress the unpleasant or dangerous features of the economic order, the government could do little. It was sounder to leave the defects of capitalists to time, and to the laws of trade and of society. For capitalists had an important function, and the ability to perform it was rare. Occasionally on this score Godkin was simply the schoolmaster reading the lesson from a textbook in elementary economics. Thus capitalists were those skilled in discerning what was needed and profitable; they secured capital either from others or from their own savings to produce or buy the desired products; and they knew how to utilize effectively the profits

20. "A Contrast Worth Notice," *Nation*, IX, 408.
21. Godkin, "Real Problems of Democracy," *Atlantic Monthly*, LXXVIII, 7.

which were their rewards. "These explorers of the race" took huge risks, for nearly ninety-five per cent failed. Luckily contemporary Darwinism was at hand to buttress such assertions. "The great capitalist is . . . gener ally a man who has been appointed by natural selection."[22] Although this gloss gave a superficial note of novelty to a somewhat hackneyed theme, Godkin showed more insight by the suggestion that America and modern business was creating a new type of capitalist or manager. Modern business, with its large-scale and complex operations, required a detailed knowledge and an instantaneousness of decision which "hardly one man in a million possessed."[23] Talent of this order was like that of the statesman. It was far greater than that required by the merchant a century earlier who could take half a year to make up his mind.

No long apprenticeship of habit and discipline trained this new American entrepreneur. He entered business young, but already equipped with a knowledge of details of many matters, with a general acquaintance with the methods of trading and of stocks and bonds, and with ambition. He did not expect to make his fortune through laborious calculations, perseverance, cautious savings, and punctuality at the office. "The prizes of commercial life—nay, even a fair amount of distinction

22. "The Great Economical Difficulty of the Day," *Nation,* XXVII, 78; Godkin, "Social Classes in the Republic," *Atlantic Monthly,* LXXVIII, 725.

23. Godkin, "Cooperation," *North American Review,* CVI, 160–161; "Democratic Tendencies," *Atlantic Monthly,* LXXIX, 158.

in it—are won by quickness of perception, activity, and courage. Five out of six of the great fortunes are made rapidly, by happy hits, or bold and ingenious combinations."[24] Daring, energy, and shrewdness were the prized business qualities. Those who had them were supposed, with luck, to be rich by forty. These traits were widespread. Even if they lacked means, the freedom and opportunity of the American economy enabled those with pluck and luck to forge ahead. American fortunes were not hereditary. The type of hero America admired was the "self-made" man, the "live man."[25]

Though in general the economic order operated beneficially or at least inevitably, matters of taste and tradition—perhaps snobbery—led Godkin to place business low in his hierarchy of values. Essentially money-making was an inferior occupation of which the wise man could neither expect nor demand much. Other occupations, like politics, literature, and art, were of a nobler order and required larger endowments from their practitioners. Besides, those who followed them were more interesting. Fighting against the admission of brokers, bankers, and merchants to the Century Club, Godkin granted they were "excellent and agreeable men" but they "rarely open a book."[26] While businessmen are apt

24. Godkin, "Commercial Immorality and Political Corruption," *North American Review*, CVII, 250.

25. Godkin, "Aristocratic Opinions of Democracy," *North American Review*, C, 218; "Commercial Immorality and Political Corruption," *North American Review*, CVII, 252; "The Democratic View of Democracy," *North American Review*, CI, 116.

26. Ogden, *op. cit.*, II, 131.

to have better taste and to pay more attention to their dress and personal cleanliness than artisans, "a very large proportion ... know no more, read no more, and have no more to say than the bricklayer and the plumber."[27]

American wealth on display, however much the public might demand and expect it, offended Godkin's deepest instincts. When Vanderbilt, whose hand "was pretty regularly in the public pocket," erected in the seventies a bronze statue of himself in the New York Central Freight Depot, Godkin was almost as angry as Moses when he found the Israelites had erected the golden calf and were dancing before it. "In short, there, in the glory of brass, are portrayed in a fashion quite good enough, the trophies of a lineal successor of the mediaeval baron that we read about, who may have been illiterate indeed; and who was not humanitarian; and not finished in his morals; and not, for his manners, the delight of the refined society of his neighborhood; nor yet beloved by his dependents."[28] Twenty years later Godkin, with less passion but with unimpaired distaste, reflected upon the craze of the American rich for great houses. These were appropriate enough in Europe where they were the centers of large landed estates and the gathering places, particularly over the long week end, of a large group with the ability to manage conversation about literature, sport, art, and politics.

27. Godkin, "Social Classes in the Republic," *Atlantic Monthly*, LXXVIII, 724.
28. "The Vanderbilt Memorial," *Nation*, IX, 430.

In their present ignorance of the "social art," America's rich couldn't swing it. "Suppose 'stocks' to be ruled out, where would the topics of conversation be found? Would there be much to talk about except the size of the host's fortune, and that of some other persons present? How many of the men would wish to sit with the ladies in the evening and participate with them in conversation?"[29] Deficiencies of this sort, though drab, were harmless enough.

Unluckily the huge sea of corporate and government securities yielded an income enabling some to live a life of "absolute leisure," free "from all distasteful labor." Since this group had to have something to do, they made a business of amusement, shuttling between resorts, beguiling themselves with tennis and polo, and finally with "the distraction of love-making under more or less illicit conditions. This is what they fall back on when all else fails or becomes vapid. . . . The worship of wealth, in its coarsest and most undraped form, too, that is, wealth as a purveyor of meat, drink, clothing, and ornamentation, which goes on in this *milieu*, 'makes hay' of all noble standards of individual and social conduct."[30] But the moralist is also disturbed lest great houses and conspicuous leisure legitimatize the envy the poor always feel for the rich. "We undoubtedly owe to suspicion and dislike of great wealth and displays

29. Godkin, "The Expenditure of Rich Men," *Scribner's Magazine*, XX, 499.

30. Godkin, "Idleness and Immorality," *Forum*, XIII, 337–340.

of it, the Bryan platform, with its absurdities and its atrocities. The accumulation of great fortunes since the war, honestly it may be, but in ways mysterious or unknown to the plain man, has introduced among us the greatest of European curses—class hatred."[31]

For in the last decade of his editorship Godkin's earlier hopes of the American experiment one by one gave way. In spite of all his talk about the universality of economic laws, he had always assumed that America would be different, and when he applied the word "European" to American policy and tendencies, he used it as an epithet. Now in the nineties all this distinction seemed destined for that oblivion which the croakers were always prophesying and he had once so buoyantly derided. Though he was suspicious of great wealth, America's fortunes, he observed in the sixties, had not led to voluptuousness nor weakened the national fibre. Now the spectacle of the idle and wanton rich confronted him. Though doubtful of money-making, he had welcomed it as a prelude, essential in a new country, to those higher attainments in intellect and in character where true progress alone was possible. Instead he saw the "immorality" of the silver movement and the unrest of an unsolved "labor craze." Most disillusioning of all was the Spanish-American War with its flare of extravagance and its aftermath of militarism and imperialism. This was the most slavish repetition of the European pattern. Of democracy he wrote to his old con-

31. Godkin, "The Expenditure of Rich Men," *Scribner's Magazine*, XX, 500.

fidant and associate, Charles Eliot Norton, "I have pretty much given it up as a contributor to the world's moral progress. . . . I, too, tremble at the thought of having a huge navy and the war-making power lodged in the hands of such puerile and thoughtless people— a hundred million strong. Morals in this community, except sexual morals, are entirely gone. . . . We all expected far too much of the human race. What stuff we used to talk."[32]

32. Godkin to Norton, August 4, 1898, November 29, 1898, Charles Eliot Norton Papers, Houghton Library, Harvard University.

-III-

THE MIRROR LOOKS
AT THE BUSINESSMAN

In the summer of 1848 the Carnegies, a family of four from Dunfermline, Scotland, debarked at New York City. Andrew Carnegie, the older of the two boys, was thirteen. In spite of the year, commonly associated with the immigration of the exceptional group of intellectuals, the forty-eighters, the Carnegies were like millions of other immigrants. They came with no letters of introduction, they were moved by no itch to observe the American experiment. Instead they were poor and they sought work. Carnegie's father had been a hand loom weaver of damasks. When machine industry at last made this skill obsolete, the Carnegies borrowed money and turned toward America as the land of opportunity. Carnegie recalls his father singing in their Dunfermline cottage:

> To the West, to the West, to the land of the free,
> Where the mighty Missouri rolls down to the sea;
> Where a man is a man even though he must toil
> And the poorest may gather the fruits of the soil.

Somewhat over half a century later Andrew Carnegie, the acknowledged iron and steel king of the United States, and his associates sold their business to the

United States Steel Corporation, the first billion dollar corporation in American history. Carnegie's share in the transaction, $250,000,000 in five per cent gold bonds in the new concern, gave him an income, according to the calculations of a reporter, of $40,000 a day. At the time of this interview there was in Carnegie's surroundings no visible symbol of this achievement. "It was the study of a litterateur or a university dean rather than the office of a steel maker from smoky Pittsburg."[1]

Both Carnegie and his biographers are fond of stressing the radicalism of his forbears and by implication of himself. No doubt the facts are there: grandfather, father, uncles were agitators against the corn laws, established churches, kings, lords, and associated privilege, and were bred on the rebellious poetry of Robert Burns. When Carnegie, in the years after he obtained fortune, often returned to the homeland for the long vacations he found both necessary and feasible, he flew over his Scottish castle "the United flag . . . the Stars and Stripes and the Union Jack sewn together—the first of that kind of flag ever seen,"[2] hobnobbed with British statesmen, addressed Scottish audiences on the virtues of home rule for Ireland, and in this ancestral setting still cut the family figure of the nonconformist. On the cover of his volume, *Triumphant Democracy*, written I suspect largely by his secretary, there is the Carnegie

1. Andrew Carnegie and Others, *Personality in Business*, The Business Man's Library, vol. 9 (Chicago: The System Company, 1907), p. 31.
2. Carnegie, "Americanism versus Imperialism," *North American Review*, CLXVIII, 6.

touch: a small golden pyramid labeled "Republic" stands firmly on its base, another golden pyramid labeled "Monarchy" stands on its point. Better than extensive quotation is the single declaratory sentence from the *Autobiography:* "Fine fellow, Rosebery, only he was handicapped by being born a peer."[3]

But in Carnegie's "Beloved Republic," America, his "extremist views" on human rights were common currency. Nor was the Carnegie creed of business so novel as to be called radical. It was conservative, perhaps even regressive. Nonetheless Carnegie was different. In a generation of businessmen supposedly incapable of appreciating anything more literary than *David Harum,* Carnegie read Bancroft, Macaulay, and Herbert Spencer. Conversation, which in the circles of high finance hardly left the solid ground of stocks, bonds, profits, losses, one's own wealth, and the wealth of one's associates, was with Carnegie heavily seasoned with quotations from Burns and Shakespeare. He not only read and quoted, he wrote. His generous output of essays is so distinctive that the student of business leadership inevitably resorts to it. His ability with the pen was so abnormal it startled even himself, as frequent embarrassed references to an author's vanity reveal. For the American businessman there is no comparable self-revelation in print.

It is not all to be taken seriously. In some of his writing, I suspect, Carnegie was simply applying the apho-

3. Carnegie, *Autobiography* (Boston: Houghton Mifflin Company, 1920), p. 311.

rism which he once recommended to clerks as a fundamental means to business advance, "HE MUST ATTRACT ATTENTION." When the "star-spangled Scotchman" advocated a crushing tariff on many luxury goods or trenchantly defended a laxer and more pleasurable observance of Sunday, he was voicing not only convictions but his desire to startle and astonish. He was sentimental. No advertiser, touched with synthetic passion, ever penned purpler tributes to mother, "honored word." As for home, "What Mecca is to the Mohammedan, Benares to the Hindoo, Jerusalem to the Christian, all that Dunfermline is to me."[4] Though he is frequently commonplace, it is easy to exaggerate the quality. To be sure, in his advice to young men on how to win business success, Carnegie's pen ran easily over the traditional banalities of thrift, energy, temperance, honesty, and "an eye single to the interests of the employer." But this partially outmoded genre, examples of which are often included in anthologies, is a booby trap even for the best minds and hardly a measure of Carnegie's thought. It would be woefully unfair, for instance, to judge the intellectual attainments of college presidents by their baccalaureate addresses. Often Carnegie was naive. Certainly the adjective was deserved for his vigorous proposal that the American tariff system punish Canada for refusing to become a republic and to join the United States, and for his belief that nations could compel arbitration and enforce the decision of a peace tribunal by refusing to associate with the offender

4. *Ibid.,* p. 318.

and by stopping the mails, a simple-minded idea even for the age of hope in which it was uttered. There was in Carnegie a touch of Henry Ford. Though all these qualities limited the value of his observations, the core of this thought was concrete and based on the soundest of premises, experience.

Carnegie believed that law governed the world of ← business. Unlike Godkin, he referred less garrulously to these overarching and controlling circumstances; unlike Adams, he did not conduct over a lifetime a disheartening quest for their discovery and statement. Like both, however, his thought on law was comparatively free from theological overtones and sanctions. Though in one place in his *Autobiography* he associates his emancipation from theology with a single revelation, actually a careful reading of the whole volume shows he had little to discard. Both his father and mother had only remnants of religion and no catechism raised or instructed their son. The battles of clerics over their different means of salvation and a trip around the world, in his case the equivalent of a course in comparative religions, convinced Carnegie that "no nation had all the truth in the revelation that it regards as divine, and no tribe is so low as to be left without some truth; . . . Buddha for one; Confucious for another; Zoroaster for a third; Christ for a fourth. The teachings of all these I found ethically akin. . . ."[5] Against the vicars on earth of a formalized and localized God he usually was content to employ an impish humor; for those who dabbled

5. *Ibid.*, p. 206.

in business and politics he added his contempt. "Ecclesiastics, . . . their attention being chiefly fixed upon the other world . . . seldom shine as advisers upon affairs pertaining to this."[6] Clearly here was in operation not natural science but the rough common sense that "the great infidel," Bob Ingersoll, was currently employing. The Unknown Power, to which he sometimes casually referred, did not provide Carnegie with law. Nor did mere secular professors of political economy. They were "writers of the closet . . . removed from personal contact with every-day affairs."[7]

Carnegie's universe of law was partly the casual parroting of vernacular phrases, as meaningless as those of an uninformed newspaper editorial: "the law of supply and demand," "the law of wages and of profits," the law of "ups and downs" in business enterprise.[8] Usually he shaped his cosmogony from observation. "The great natural laws," he concluded, were "the outgrowth of human nature and human needs."[9] These human urges sired siblings: the law of competition and the law of the aggregation of capital and establishments. Far from being contradictory, these two laws operated in a sort of moving tension to produce a beneficent equilibrium. The law of competition prevented the formation of

6. Carnegie, "Americanism versus Imperialism," *The Gospel of Wealth*, p. 195.

7. Carnegie, "Results of the Labor Struggle," *ibid.*, p. 127.

8. Carnegie, *Empire of Business* (New York: Doubleday, Page & Company, 1902), pp. 84, 119.

9. Carnegie, "Popular Illusions about Trusts," *Gospel of Wealth*, p. 102.

trusts. Once these great enterprises were established and prices raised, outsiders would be tempted by the prize and invade the favored field of production. They in turn might consolidate; in turn new competitors would arise. "Such is the law, such has been the law, and such promises to be the law for the future."[10] On its part the great law of the aggregation of capital and the enlargement of plant introduced that large-scale production which lowered prices and thus contributed to the enrichment of the masses. This second law would not result in monopoly, for the former law, the law of competition, prevented such an outcome. Syndicates were obsolete and trusts, at best only a "bugaboo," would soon be out of fashion.

Although he had rejected the determinism of Presbyterian theology, Carnegie's laws of business were irresistible and inexorable. They could no more be thwarted than "the laws of nature which determine the humidity of the atmosphere or the revolution of the earth upon its axis." Nonetheless his business operations at times seemed to challenge law—apparently without punishment. Though he was certain in print that "these grand, immutable, all-wise laws of natural forces" worked perfectly "if human legislators would only let them alone" and regretted that "our governors, all over the world, are at Sisyphus's work—ever rolling the stone uphill to see it roll back to its proper bed at the bottom,"[11] he

10. Carnegie, *Empire of Business*, p. 161.
11. Carnegie, *Triumphant Democracy* (New York: Charles Scribner's Sons, 1886), p. 48.

was willing to advocate in print a protective tariff for infant industries and laws restricting the hours of labor. Perhaps these exceptions in practice or statement revealed that the laws had been inadequately stated, or had been forgotten, or had been ignored through that necessity which, we are informed, knows no law. Be that as it may, "the laws of natural forces" were not universally beneficent. Their operation resulted in hardship and loss for individuals, and great inequalities in the accumulation of wealth. They so widened the gap between the employer and employee that the latter became a "machine" in the eyes of the former and the former a "myth" in the eyes of the latter. Labor hostility and strife were the result.

Still the gains outweighed the losses and the evil was sometimes good. Herbert Spencer, clad in the armor of evolution, came to the rescue. In the course of reading several volumes by his "great teacher" and one by Darwin, Carnegie reached the pages which explain how "man has absorbed such mental foods as were favorable to him, retaining what was salutary, rejecting what was deleterious, [so that] light came as in a flood and all was clear.... I had found the truth of evolution. 'All is well since all grows better' became my motto, my true source of comfort."[12] Whether or not this simplification embodied the whole truth of Darwin or Spencer, the vernacular of their ideas gave a fashionable tone to the Carnegie vision. He relished the chummy phrase, "we evolutionists," warmed himself before the comfortable

12. Carnegie, *Autobiography*, p. 339.

fire of "the survival of the fittest," and discovered that the great law of aggregation of capital was "an evolution from the heterogeneous to the homogeneous, and is clearly another step in the upward path of development."[13] Though these reassuring verbalisms give the impression of thought, Carnegie's philosophy on this matter of high moment was more glandular than intellectual. Sanguine, buoyant, and successful, he was an optimist by instinct.

While the geniality of this approach, coupled with personal factors, often led Carnegie into a misguided appraisal of the Gilded Age, it was no more fallible than the pessimism of Adams or the anxiety of Godkin. The year 1886 was a test of whether an observer could keep his head and formulate sound judgments. Strikes sputtered on every side. The Knights of Labor, the first massive, centralized labor organization in American history, attained a membership of over 700,000 and convinced a newspaper editor that the power of the President and Cabinet over the Army, Navy, and the Civil Service was "petty" compared to that possessed by the five leaders of the Knights. "They can stay the nimble touch of almost every telegraph operator, can shut up most of the mills and factories, and can disable the railroads." There was a national movement for the eight-hour day. In May when the police were dispersing a labor protest meeting in Haymarket Square in Chicago, a bomb killed several police and a group of anarchist

13. Carnegie, "Popular Illusions about Trusts," *The Gospel of Wealth,* p. 89.

agitators was forthwith arrested and tried. Four were hanged for murder. Hysteria was at every side. Into this excitement, Carnegie moved with a magazine article. It was hardly likely that he would exonerate the anarchists. On the other hand he dissipated the current alarm over a "social revolt" by the careful use of statistics, discussed the demands and methods of labor organizations with perception and sympathy, and calmly stressed the "indestructability of human society." The sanity and serenity of the "evolutionist" here stood him in good stead.

Equally refreshing was his frank celebration of the businessman. As a prelude to his enthusiasm he was careful to define what he meant by that designation. The businessman was not the technician, the engineer, or the able machinist—though he might have their qualities. The businessman was not the speculator. On this theme Carnegie was eloquent. Speculating on the stock exchange was gambling. Fascinated by the ups and downs of the market, the speculator was too preoccupied with the vacillating values of securities to pay attention to his business. A reputation for speculation weakened the businessman's credit rating. Since it created nothing, speculation was antisocial. As for the promoter and the banker, Carnegie was somewhat less specific. On the whole their legerdemain was not to his taste. "They throw cats and dogs together and call them elephants," he once exclaimed. Their stockwatering and extravagant valuations brought about losses to the investor. Coupling his general criteria with such hints as he drops, I conclude Carnegie would have condemned Fisk and Gould, reserved judgment on J. P. Morgan, and perhaps permitted Junius Morgan to enter his pantheon. The last was an "old-fashioned banker" with a sense of honor. "The type has become rare," observed Carnegie in his *Autobiography*. The businessman of whom Carnegie approved was the "merchant" and the "maker." "I wished to make something tangible and sell it. . . . The true gold mine lies right in their own factories."[14]

But admission to this hallowed area was not enough. The receiver of a salary was not a businessman. No matter how great his responsibility or his recompense, he was a servant. "Strictly speaking . . . a man, to be in business, must be at least part owner of the enterprise which he manages and to which he gives his attention, and chiefly dependent for his revenues not upon salary but upon its profits. . . . The business man pure and simple plunges into and tosses upon the waves of human affairs without a life-preserver in the shape of salary; he risks all."[15] With this concept of the businessman as the innovator, the risk-taker, the self-employed, Carnegie naturally cherished a deep suspicion of the corporate form of organization. Although he occasionally declared that like the trust and the monopoly, it was on the way to disappearance, he more frequently endeavored to prove that even within the shelter of its forms, a handful of individuals with interest in the firm were

14. Carnegie, *Autobiography*, pp. 176, 177.
15. Carnegie, *Empire of Business*, pp. 189–190.

really responsible for its business success. He preferred, of course, the partnership. No clutter of directors had to be consulted, no army of absentee and uninformed stockholders lurked darkly over the horizon. A partnership could work with speed. By offering men with technical and managerial ability but without financial resources a share in the partnership which they could eventually buy from the profits in the enterprise, incentive joined talent in irresistible combination. "How would you like to be a millionaire?" Carnegie asked his potential "young geniuses." For business talent was not hereditary. It developed largely from the poor boy who started in business by sweeping out the office in the morning. The American business man was the self-made man.

In his estimation a genuine talent for innovation and enterprise was rare. According to figures which he loved to repeat, 95 per cent of those who tried business failed. So precious, indeed, was this power for business success that Carnegie momentarily dallied with the idea that business ability might even conquer inexorable law. In one of his sanguine demonstrations that trusts were on the way to limbo, the obvious success of the Standard Oil group gave him pause. Clearly this achievement would have been impossible if the Standard Oil Company had not been "managed, upon the whole, in harmony with the laws which control business." Its position of mastery, however, challenged in the most disturbing way the law of competition. This dilemma Carnegie met by a tribute to the "genius at its head, a commander-in-chief, with exceptionally able corps commanders no doubt, but still a Grant at the head,"[16] and the prophecy that with Rockefeller's retirement dissolution would set in.

By the simple act of narrowing his definition of the businessman, Carnegie eased his task of expounding and defending the contemporary business world. Within the area he had chosen, however, he was sure that there *Business Value* were justifications for his calling. One was the social. ←
The businessman developed natural resources, gave employment to thousands of workers, and by quickening and cheapening production brought new comforts, enjoyments, and more of the luxuries of the rich, including "more sweetness and light," to the "toiling millions." In moments of crisis, the business leader stood ←
ready to aid his nation. Furthermore business benefited ←
its practitioners. As he informed the undergraduates of Cornell, "I can confidently recommend to you the business career as one in which there is abundant room for the exercise of man's highest power, and of every good quality in human nature. I believe the career of the great merchant, or banker, or captain of industry, to be favourable to the development of the powers of the mind, and to the ripening of the judgement upon a wide range of general subjects; to freedom from prejudice, and the keeping of an open mind.... The business career is thus a stern school of all the virtues."[17] Yet for all its romance, breadth, and righteousness, business had

16. *Ibid.*, pp. 158–159.
17. *Ibid.*, p. 224.

one fatal defect. Though the great merchants and manufacturers might ultimately free themselves from it, the chief aim of business was money-making. This was both ignoble and sordid. At the end Carnegie joined Adams and Godkin.

It was not because he saw in other occupations a nobler expression of human ability or because he was willing to place politics, art, and the professions higher in the hierarchy of values. They were different rather than superior. On the basis of observation and experience, conceivably in this instance so narrow that Carnegie did not know what he was talking about, he concluded that the artist in music, painting, or sculpture with his hunger for fame was inspired by motives less ignoble than a desire for material wealth. Nonetheless as a class artists were not highly educated, lacked the "all-around brain," and were prone to "a narrow, selfish, personal vanity" and other "petty passions." Professional men lacked vanity and pettiness. Still their specialization, as contrasted with the generalized and world-wide views of the businessman, made "what is known as the professional mind, clear, but narrow."[18]

For the college-educated man, Carnegie exhibited a tempered enthusiasm. In view of the thousands of libraries he scattered over the world and his endowments and gifts to colleges and universities, the attitude is surprising. Nonetheless Carnegie's observation led him to conclude that a college education was not essential for winning a fortune and might be a positive handicap.

18. *Ibid.*, pp. 146, 216, 218.

For one thing it delayed the start in the race for business success; the future prize-gatherers, sweeping out the office, had already left the starting mark in their teens. A college education was likely to inculcate bad habits, a slackening in effort, concentration, ambition, and self-discipline. The contemporary curriculum was wrong. "Men have sent their sons to colleges to waste their energies upon obtaining a knowledge of such languages as Greek and Latin, which are of no more practical use to them than Choctaw. ... They have been crammed with the details of petty and insignificant skirmishes between savages, and taught to exalt a band of ruffians into heroes. ... They have been 'educated' as if they were destined for life upon some other planet than this."[19] Carnegie sometimes modified his indictment, perhaps when he was addressing a university audience or when he admitted the necessity of education for those who were entering the professions or preparing for a life of leisure and well-doing. If the curriculum were reformed to include natural science, engineering, and Shakespeare, whose works Carnegie had mastered, much could be forgiven. The truth of the matter is that he made a distinction between reading and education. The individualistic self-help of the former process, a process through which he had traveled, appealed to him. He preferred the self-educated as well as the self-made man.

Nor did religion convince him that wealth was sin. In spite of his theological emancipation, he knew the Bibli-

19. *Ibid.*, pp. 79–90.

cal arguments against great riches, and "that little white-haired Scotch devil of mine,"[20] as one of his first employers described him, could quote Scripture with the best of them. The hard saying, "It is easier for a camel to enter the eye of a needle than for a rich man to enter the kingdom of heaven," he modified, by verbal exegesis and the warning that it was not to be understood literally, just enough so that he could use it against the religious-minded rich as an argument for his own "Gospel of Wealth." Far more to his taste was the parable of the talents. "It was those who had accumulated, and even doubled their capital to whom the Lord said: 'Well done, thou good and faithful servant: thou hast been faithful over a few things, I will make thee ruler over many things: enter thou into the joy of thy Lord.'"[21]

Rather than religion or learning, it was the admiration of poverty that made Carnegie distrust wealth. The life of honest poverty best taught the virtues of effort and struggle. Poverty was a bracing school. It was poverty, the equal start, that most fitted with Carnegie's ingrained dislike of privilege, that inequality that had "insulted" him from birth. It was poverty that made parents rear and train their children. "This is where the children of honest poverty have the most precious advantages over those of wealth. The mother, nurse, cook, governess, teacher, saint, all in one; the father, exemplar, guide, counselor, and friend! Thus

20. Carnegie, *Autobiography*, p. 72.
21. Carnegie, "The Advantages of Poverty," *The Gospel of Wealth*, p. 74.

were my brother and I brought up. What has the child of millionaire or nobleman that counts compared to such a heritage?"[22] Historically the great, the good, and the genius had almost always fought upward from the lowest ranks. The resulting dilemma was clear to Carnegie: that individuals should acquire wealth was inevitable and desirable, its inheritance injured the next generation. Less sentimental observers had faced the same dichotomy. Decades earlier John Adams had asked how superior talent and ability could avoid acquiring wealth and how the acquisition of wealth could avoid causing luxury and vice.

To this age-old query Carnegie made answer with his secular gospel of wealth. Rich men should neither transmit their fortunes to their descendants nor bequeath them for public purposes. It was their responsibility and duty to distribute their dollars in their lifetime, to administer personally their property as a trust for society. They would bring to this task of philanthropy the talents which had enabled them to make money. In short they would do for the community more wisely than the community could do for itself. Whatever the *non sequiturs* of the argument, Carnegie lived up to his principles in relentless fashion. That the application of the gospel would transform the gospeler was certain: "Whether the millionaire wishes it or not, he cannot evade the law which under present conditions, compels him to use his millions for the good of the people. All that he gets during the few years of his life is that he may live in a finer house, surround himself with finer

22. Carnegie, *Autobiography*, p. 31.

furniture.... He can eat richer food and drink richer wines.... But truly the modern millionaire is generally a man of very simple tastes and even miserly habits. He spends little upon himself, and is the toiling bee laying up the honey in the industrial hive, which all the inmates of that hive, the community in general, will certainly enjoy.... Under our present conditions the millionaire who toils on is the cheapest article which the community secures at the price it pays for him, namely, his shelter, clothing, and food.... It will be a great mistake for the community to shoot the millionaires."[23] As a statement of law or a picture of contemporary actuality, not excluding a self-portrait, fancy could go no further.

Here was one of the times when, for all his shrewdness and practicality, Carnegie was the wishful thinker. There were other occasions—as his theories of corporations, trusts, and competition have demonstrated. But few, whether radical or conservative, can survey the future without error; all we can demand is insight into the present. Carnegie held the mirror up to business. What he saw was himself. That reflection was in large measure a reflection of the past. Here, not too dimly seen, was the self-employed handicraftsman of Dunfermline, translated to America and blown great by the possession of millions.

WHILE ONLY the simplifier would claim that Adams, Godkin, and Carnegie were typical, they at least con-

23. Carnegie, *Empire of Business*, pp. 136, 137, 138, 140.

stituted a body of conservative opinion in the Gilded Age. Their conclusion that the business order of their day was not all evil, loss, and hypocrisy should con- tribute to a more balanced judgment of the era. They were not complacent. Like the radicals, they saw the practices, many of them shameful, and problems, most of them complex, arising from a period of exceptionally rapid change. Though they were in varied degrees perplexed as to what course to follow, they were certain that solutions must accord with first principles and fundamental laws. All this may well seem quaint, fruitless, and perhaps somehow ludicrous to a generation whose most popular statesman asserted that economic laws were made by men and that the people had learned how to control blind economic forces. On their part the conservatives of the Gilded Age doubted that they, unaided and uninstructed by law, had either the requisite omniscience to select goals or the omnipotence to attain them. For them it was far from clear that reason guided men or that men could control their environment. Perhaps their limitations were their strength.